Oxford Secondary English

Teacher's Book 2

John Seely

Oxford
University
Press
1982

Oxford University Press, Walton Street, Oxford OX2 6DP

London   Glasgow   New York   Toronto
Delhi   Bombay   Calcutta   Madras   Karachi
Nairobi   Dar es Salaam   Salisbury   Cape Town
Kuala Lumpur   Singapore   Hong Kong   Tokyo
Melbourne   Auckland

and associate companies in
Beirut   Berlin   Ibadan   Mexico City

© Oxford University Press 1982
ISBN 0 19 831136 2

Photoset in Great Britain by
Rowland Phototypesetting Ltd,
Bury St Edmunds, Suffolk
and printed by Cambridge University Press, Cambridge.

Contents

Introduction

General

The best English teaching is done by teachers who know the children in their classes and choose materials and activities suited to their needs at the time. During any term their work together is very varied. This necessitates knowledge, experience, and sensitivity on the part of the teacher. It also requires time: time to think, to select, to prepare.

Unfortunately time is limited. This is particularly true for the teacher who is conscientious about reading and commenting on what his classes write. In addition, on many occasions teachers are asked to take responsibility for teaching English when it is not their specialist subject. For such 'part-time' English teachers the variety of possibilities and practice may seem bewildering.

In this course we have tried to offer a variety of materials in a form that will appeal to the children; but at the same time provide a structure that gives the teacher support, guidance, and choice in the business of organizing a coherent programme of work.

So, instead of the conventional one book per year, there are two: one for the pupils and one for the teacher. The pupil's book contains all the source materials plus some work assignments. The teacher's book contains most of the work assignments, as well as guidance on the use of the materials.

The books are divided into two sections. Section A, by far the larger, contains a selection of prose, poetry, and visual material grouped into nine themes. There are also three 'Specials'. Section B focusses on specific aspects of written communication.

The use of two books has great advantages. Putting most of the work assignments from Section A in the teacher's book frees the pupil's book for a really solid selection of source material. It also means that we can avoid burdening every piece of writing with the inevitable set of questions or writing assignment. The children only 'have to do work' on a particular item, if the teacher feels that it is appropriate. Otherwise the poem, extract or picture is simply there in its own right. More material means more choice. The teacher's book contains a greater variety of assignments, *at different levels*, than is normally possible. This means that the teacher can choose work that suits the needs and *abilities* of his class.

The division into two sections is intended to give the teacher control over when to deal with specific skills. When do you focus on the punctuation of direct speech? 'When the children are ready and need it,' says the teacher. 'In Chapter 6, during the spring term,' says the traditional course book. The teacher needs to be able to choose when this type of work is done. Placing it in a second section makes this possible.

ANALYSIS OF THE MATERIALS

Pupil's book

The pupil's book is divided into two sections:

1   Section A: 9 thematic units, averaging 14 pages each
              3 special units, averaging 10 pages each
2   Section B: 15 skills units, of 2 pages each

Teacher's book

The teacher's book is divided into three sections:

1   Introduction
2   Section A: Divided up in a similar way to the pupil's book, and
    containing the majority of the assignments on the source material
    in the pupil's book, as well as a variety of teaching notes.
3   Section B: Short teaching notes on the materials in Section B of the
    pupil's book.

Using a thematic unit

Each thematic unit is arranged in the same way. Occasionally there may
be minor variations from the pattern presented here. Each thematic unit
is designed to contain sufficient material for about three weeks' work.

Page 1: **Title**:   One or more illustrations introducing the theme as a
whole. These can be used for a brief introductory discussion. A few
discussion points are usually suggested at the foot of the page.

Pages 2–3: **Lead story**:   Usually a passage of prose fiction, presenting
one aspect of the theme in a striking or dramatic way.
Followed by: *Questions to think and talk about*
               Writing

This double page spread is intended for use in the first one or two
lessons on the new theme. Sometimes the teacher's book contains supplementary material on these pages.

Pages 4–5: **Comprehension**:   One or two pages of comprehension
and writing, usually based on factual prose. Supplementary material of
varying grades of difficulty is usually provided in the teacher's book.
This is particularly useful for work with mixed-ability classes.

Since the comprehension material extends the theme in a different
direction from the Lead Story, it can be used immediately after it, left
until later, or omitted.

Pages 6–12: **Sources**:   A wide variety of prose, verse, and illustrations
developing the theme. All activities based on this material are in the
teacher's book. They are written in the form of direct address to the
pupil and can therefore be used without further preparation by the
teacher who simply has to duplicate them, write them on the black-
board, or just read them to the pupils.

This device frees the pupil's book for more source material. It leaves
the teacher free to decide which material will be developed in detail. It
frees the pupils from the requirements of a set of questions or writing

assignment after everything they read. Some of the source material can simply be read for pleasure.

Pages 13–14: **Puzzles**:   A number of exercises and word puzzles related to the theme. These can be used to fill odd moments, or set for homework.

This material also includes further comprehension work, usually in the form of cloze or sequencing exercises.

Using a special unit

The Specials are not based on themes. They are extended projects in writing, or writing, talking, and drama. (The same material can be used in different ways.) They can be used by individuals, or the class can work on them in groups. With many classes it should be possible for pupils to work for longish periods of time without intervention from the teacher. The responsibility of self-directed work is good for the pupil; it also provides occasions when the teacher is free to give individual pupils attention in more depth than is usually the case. Many teachers will welcome the opportunities offered by these units particularly at the end of term. *Full instructions for these units are placed in the pupil's book.*

Using a skills unit

The skills units can be used in one of two ways:
  for class teaching
  for individual reference and practice

Each unit is composed in the same way:
  left-hand page: reference data
  right-hand page: exercises

The only exceptions to this are the last two units which consist of lists of spelling rules and difficult words.

SPECIFIC ACTIVITIES

Talking

One of the most important ways in which we learn is through talking and listening to other people. Speech is not just an important means of gathering and conveying information, it is a fundamental way in which our mental picture of the world is constantly being adjusted. In the past schools have failed to take full notice of this. In the traditional classroom most of the talking is done by the teacher while the pupils' role is to listen. As a result, most classrooms are still arranged in a way that discourages the kind of talk that leads to real learning. Such talk is exploratory, tentative, informal. The traditional classroom is designed for formal question-and-answer work.

This means that the teacher has to overcome a certain inertia if he is to have useful talk going on in his classroom. The problems that may exist can be set out thus:

Problems deriving from the school
1   Other teachers may disapprove: they may feel that talk is not 'work'.
2   Senior teachers may officially discourage talk, since they consider that it leads to disorder.
3   The arrangement of the classrooms may make informal talk difficult to get going.

Problems deriving from the teacher
4   He may worry that some children will 'take advantage' of the informality to misbehave.
5   He may feel that he cannot adequately monitor what is going on during informal talk.
6   He may feel under pressure to produce written work in every lesson.

Problems deriving from the pupils
7   If the method is little used in the school they may be uncertain of how to behave.
8   If the teacher seems unsure of himself they may reflect his nervousness in their classroom behaviour.

The teacher has to work within the school. He must decide for himself how best to cope with the prevailing 'official' opinion about talk. The remaining problems are more apparent than real. With determination, confidence and good planning, they can be overcome. It is possible to structure lessons in such a way that everyone knows clearly where he stands and what he has to do. Once he has started, the teacher will soon see the real benefits that the children are deriving from informal talk as these begin to spill over into all the other activities of English lessons.

Working in small groups
Without doubt the most effective method of organizing this kind of learning is in small groups. Initially a lot of very useful work can be done in pairs, with the teacher simply instructing members of the class to discuss the topic with the person they are sitting next to. Some pairs, however, do not get on, for one reason or another, so often a slightly larger group – of four or even, on occasions, five – proves more satisfactory in the long run. Such group discussion, when properly managed by the teacher, is in fact often more productive (and less wearing) than the more conventional class discussion with the teacher acting as chairman.

Arranging the groups
Some teachers simply tell the children to 'get into groups', allowing them to do so simply on a basis of friendship. Others go to the opposite extreme and construct elaborately artificial and balanced groups that

take no account of the preferences of the children involved. Probably something between the two is the most successful: the children propose and the teacher disposes. Its organization may seem a little complicated, but is well worthwhile.

1 The teacher explains to the class what is going to be done: they will be working in small groups and they are to have some choice about whom they will work with.
2 Each child is given a piece of paper. He writes on it: his own name, followed by the names of the four people he would most like to work with in English. This is done without discussion, and in secrecy.
3 The teacher collects the papers which can then be used to guide his construction of the working groups. Children can be grouped mainly according to friendship (which is, after all, a very important criterion) but the teacher can ensure that the groups are balanced in ability. He can also avoid having all the 'old lags' in one group.
4 At the next lesson the children are told their groups. Both they and the teacher have had a say in how the groups are made up. In theory at least, everyone is happy.

Organizing group work
The most important factor contributing to the success of small group discussion is simple, but often overlooked: every member of every group must have a very clear idea of what he is expected to do. This can be reduced to three fairly simple questions:

1 How are we to organize ourselves?
2 Exactly what are we supposed to be talking about?
3 What is the outcome supposed to be?

In the early stages it is advisable to tell each group to appoint a chairman (or to appoint one yourself.) The chairman's job is to ensure that the group sticks to the point and to resolve any disputes about whose turn it is to speak – if they are that sort of group.

Inexperienced groups find it helpful to have a list of topics or questions which are to be covered. The *Discussion points* in the teacher's book materials for Section A are presented with this in mind.

A simple way of monitoring group work 'in advance' is to tell the groups that after a given period they are going to have to report back to the rest of the class, either by giving their answers to a set of questions, or by reporting the conclusions they reached. Another role for the chairman can then be to record decisions.

This kind of formal organization is particularly useful early on. As children become accustomed to this method of working it will often be found that there is no need for such a structure. Some classes, on the other hand, will always need it.

Monitoring

Teachers who are new to this kind of work are often uncertain of their own role once the discussion has begun. There are all the children busily talking away: what do I do now? How do I make sure that they aren't talking about something completely different? Such worries are usually unfounded (and illogical: after all, how do you make sure that any particular child is actually reading silently when he is supposed to be?). The way in which the teacher has set things up nearly always ensures that most of the time most of the children will be doing what he wants them to do. If they are not, then they are probably not just talking about something else, they are probably actively disrupting the rest of the class. In that case it is the teacher's relationship with the class that is at fault and not the teaching method itself.

If you do not know the class well, it is probably unhelpful to walk round and try to join in particular discussions. It is better to choose two or three 'observation points' in the room from which you can 'tune in' to the talk of the groups around you, without making it particularly obvious that you are doing so. When you do know the class well, it is both valuable and enjoyable to be able to join in particular discussions.

The teacher's most important function, however, is probably to assess how the session as a whole is going. He needs to be able to judge when the talk is beginning to flag and to intervene, either by bringing things to a conclusion or by introducing some new element. This is the most difficult thing to learn about managing group discussion.

Working with the whole class

Some teachers will prefer to work fairly frequently, or even all the time, with the class as a whole. Those who do should try to achieve the best elements of small group discussion in their work with the class.

1   The role of the teacher

He should avoid being too 'heavy' and should encourage children to talk directly to each other rather than always speaking 'through' him. Ideally he should just be there to cue in individuals who are looking for a chance to contribute.

2   Informality

As far as possible it is important to avoid the heavily structured pattern of   teacher-talks-class-listen-then-pupil-answers-teacher-comments. This is partly done by the teacher disciplining himself to listen to what children actually say, rather than looking for what he thinks they ought to be saying. It is helped by not interrupting children more often than necessary. Most of all it is done by the teacher keeping quiet.

3   Participation

The aim should always be to have as many children as possible actively participating. It is a useful (and sobering) exercise after a class discussion for the teacher to ask himself:

a For what proportion of the total time was *I* talking?
b What percentage of the children spoke?

(This is not to say that just because a child does not speak he is not participating. There is such a thing as active listening.)

Using the materials
Every unit of Section A contains three types of material that can lead to oral work.

1 *Questions about a passage or poem*
The *Starter* questions are always of this kind. Other sets of questions in the teacher's book may be suitable. Such material can be used for group work or taken with a whole class.

2 *Discussion points*
These are particularly useful as guidelines for small group discussion, but they can also be used with the class together.

3 *Group work*
Here the instructions in the teacher's book are written in the form of address *to groups*. It is usually difficult or impossible to use this material in any other way.

Drama
The drama materials contained in Section A of the teacher's book do not of themselves provide a sustained or coherent programme of work in drama for a year. They are not intended to. They are designed to supplement work already being done in drama, whether by the English teacher or by a drama specialist. Teachers who are inexperienced in this type of work and who feel that they would like to begin it, are recommended to use some of the early materials in *Dramakit* (John Seely, Oxford University Press).

Every thematic unit does contain one or more items of drama work. They take various forms:

Role-play: in which the participants are invited to take on social roles in a situation related to the theme. In such situations, the participants can still use quite a lot of their own personalities – they do not have to go very far towards constructing a 'character'.

Playmaking: in which instructions are given (normally for groups) explaining how to set about constructing one or more scenes expressing a reaction to a situation, character or theme. Such scenes may or may not ultimately be shared with the rest of the class.

'Radio' plays: from time to time either role-play work (especially on interviews) or script-writing exercises lead naturally to the construction of 'radio' plays. If there are enough tape recorders available then plays can be recorded, which is clearly the most satisfactory

arrangement. If not, then the plays can be prepared for a live per-formance.

There are, too, occasionally suggestions for the organization of more complex and detailed drama lessons. In these cases specific advice is provided for the teacher.

Comprehension

There are three main types of comprehension exercise offered in this book:

a   conventional questions
b   cloze procedure
c   sequencing

It is our belief that *all* comprehension work benefits from being done by pairs or in small groups. This is particularly true, however, of cloze and sequencing tests.

In cloze tests one is asking the reader(s) to see into the mind of the writer and work out by inner or outer discussion what word he would have put into the blank spaces that have been left in the text. (For those unaccustomed to the techniques, there are examples of cloze tests on pages 43 and 120 of the pupil's book). In some cases there is only one possible answer, especially if the missing word is a structural word – for example a conjunction, an article or a pronoun. In others there is a range of choice. The range goes from words that are more or less interchangeable with the original word to those that could just fit the space but which are really rather unlikely. The point is that all these possibilities should be *discussed*: it is not just a question of the teacher's announcing the right answers.

In sequencing tests, discussion is again very valuable. The scope for disagreement is of course much smaller. Normally there is one correct order and that is the end of it. On the other hand there are occasionally segments of the text that could appear in a different order from that of the original. Here again is fine scope for worthwhile discussion of how a piece of writing is actually *made*.

Contents

COURAGE

* Pupil's book page
** Teacher's book page

Analysis of activities

Discussion: 1   3   6   T4   T6   T7
Writing: newspaper report   T3
          personal   3
          letter   T4
          poetry   T5
Comprehension: sequencing   5
                questions   T3
Problem solving: 5
Group work: T4
Drama: use of dialogue   T5
          role-play   T3
Language in use: newspapers   T6

Illustration

Pupil's book page **1**   role-play

Role-play
A *Solo*
You are a professional relief worker aiding the victims of this disaster.
You have a number of voluntary helpers. They have no previous
experience and you have to tell them everything that has to be done.
How would you advise them to help each of the people in these pictures?
Study the pictures carefully and decide what your approach would be.

B *Pairs*
1 Decide who is A and who is B. A – professional relief worker.
  B – volunteer helper.
2 B – choose one of the people in the pictures. Look at the person
  carefully. Now go to A and tell A about this person.
3 A – advise B how to help the person that he has told you about.

C *Pairs*
1 A – voluntary helper. B – victim.
2 Now A is going to try to help the disaster victim that you have been
  talking about. Before you begin: A – decide what you will say first;
  B – decide what your main worry is and what you are thinking.
3 When you are both ready, begin the conversation.

Keep hold of yourself

Pupil's book pages **2–3**   comprehension

Questions
This extract comes from a longer story. These questions ask you to
think about the story as a whole as well as the part you have read. In
many cases there is more than one possible answer.
1 What sort of day was it when Lennie was bitten by the snake?
2 What do you think had happened to Lennie's father?
3 What is a diner?
4 Why were Lennie and his mother living at the diner?
5 Why were they going to have to move?
6 What impression do you get of Lennie's mother?
7 How do you think Lennie felt towards his mother?

These questions, which require the reader to think and speculate about
the story can be used to deepen the class response to the immediate
situation. They are more suitable for oral answer (after a period for
individual or small group work) than for written response – although
oral work could be followed by some kind of writing.

3

Children against the jungle

Pupil's book pages **4–5**

Group work   (Groups of 4 or 5)
You are the survivors of the crash. You have a series of problems:

1   Kathy
2   Hunger
3   Thirst
4   Direction-finding
5   The jungle

You have a small amount of food and equipment:

1   5 small chocolate bars
2   1 packet of raisins
3   2 machetes (curved, heavy knives)
4   A revolver
5   Whatever you had in your pockets when the plane crashed

What to do:

1   Decide who is who. The main characters are: Oscar, Grace, Kathy.
2   Decide how to solve each of your problems.
3   Decide on a version of what happens to you, so that you can tell your story to the rest of the class.

This expanded version of the *Problem* in the pupil's book can be used like this – as a discussion and reporting back session. Alternatively the groups can be set to solve the problems (but *not* make up a complete story.) The teacher can then extend the story by adding fresh incidents as the story progresses: snake bite, illness, tropical storm, etc.

Writing
You are one of the survivors. When you get back to safety you write a letter to a friend describing your ordeal.

Wrong order: answers
The correct sequence is: 3 – 5 – 7 – 1 – 6 – 4 – 2

Using your own ideas

The first extract is from a poem by D. H. Lawrence. The second is from
I'm the King of the Castle by Susan Hill. The Lawrence poem continues:

They would distil the essential oil out of every experience
and like hazel-nuts in autumn, at last
be sweet and sound.
And the young among the old
would be as in the hazel-woods of September
nutting, gathering nuts of ripe experience.
As it is, all that the old can offer
is sour, bitter fruits, cankered by lies.

The extracts can simply be used for discussion, using the questions in
the pupil's book, or they may be used for writing and drama, as below.

Writing: Courage
These words are the beginning of a thought poem, in which the writer
gives his thoughts about courage and truth. Think about how he
begins. Then write your own continuation to the poem.

Drama: In the wood
Pairs or small groups
1   Read the passage through two or three times.
2   Discuss it and decide the answers to these questions:
    How many people are involved?
    Who are they?
    What is happening?
    How did they get there?
3   Cast the parts.
4   You are going to act the scene, but there is no need to use the exact
    words printed. Decide how the scene should begin, but *not* how it
    ends. Get ready to start.
5   When you are all ready go through the scene.
6   When you have finished, discuss what you did and whether you are
    satisfied with it. You may wish to go through the scene again.

Martin Luther King

Pupil's book pages **7–9**

Questions to think and talk about

1 Why did the Negroes in Montgomery boycott the buses?
2 Was Martin Luther King brave to take on the Presidency of the M.I.A.?
3 In his speech he said that the Negro Rights movement was completely different from the Ku Klux Klan. Was it?
4 What were the effects of the bomb attack on the Kings' house?
5 Was Martin Luther King a brave man? In what ways did he show it in the passage printed here?
6 What did King believe about the use of violence? Do you agree with him?

Note: The photograph shows the King family saying grace before a meal.

Language in use

Newspapers present news in different ways according to the beliefs of their owners and editors. Here are two invented headlines that might have appeared the day after the attack on the Kings' house:

BLACKS RIOT AFTER BOMB/KING CALMS ANGRY CROWD

Copy each headline and after it write a paragraph describing the event in the way that paper might have done.

When you have finished, compare your two versions. Ask yourself these questions:

1 Are they different?
2 Do they show different political beliefs?
3 How are they different?
4 How do they show the beliefs of their writers and editors?

This work can lead in to more detailed discussion and examination of newspapers and the way in which they present the news. On the other hand, such writing and discussion requires some maturity and it may be preferable to leave it until later.

The shed

Pupil's book pages **10–12**   discussion

It is useful to introduce the passage with some general talk, either in small groups, or with the class as a whole, about the nature of fear and what it is like to be frightened.

Introductory questions

1   What sort of thing makes people of your age frightened?
2   Would you find it frightening to be shut in somewhere and be unable to get out?
3   Would it make any difference if the place was dark?
4   Has anything like that ever happened to you?
5   When people *are* frightened in situations like that, what are they frightened of?
6   Where do these fears come from?

Follow-up questions

1   How would you describe the way Kingshaw approached the shed?
2   Why was he like this?
3   Who locked the door?
4   Why?
5   Why did Kingshaw get so scared?
6   Why did he fall asleep?

Puzzles

Pupil's book pages **13–14**   answers

Jumbled sentences

1D   2A   3C   4E   5B

1   She was a Jewish girl who had to hide from the Nazis and kept a diary describing her experiences. (Anne Frank)
2   She was an Ancient Briton who led her followers against the Romans but was defeated and killed herself. (Boudicca)
3   He was a fighter pilot in the Battle of Britain but was very badly wounded so he devoted his life to helping handicapped people. (Group-captain Leonard Cheshire, V.C.)
4   He wanted to be the first man to reach the South Pole but he failed and died before he could reach safety. (Captain Robert Scott)
5   She devoted her life to making life better for women in prison. (Elizabeth Fry)

Extensions

Further Reading

Fiction Prose

Ashley, B.	*Terry on the Fence*
Byars, B.	*The TV Kid*
	The Eighteenth Emergency
Christopher, J.	*The Guardians*
	The Prince in Waiting
Cooper, S.	*The Dawn of Fear*
Godden, R.	*The Diddakoi*
Hill, S.	*I'm the King of the Castle*
Holm, A.	*I Am David*
Kipling, R.	*The Man Who Would Be King*
Lingard, J.	*Across the Barricades*
Maddock, R.	*The Pit*
Schaefer, J.	*Shane*
	The Canyon
Southall, I.	*Ash Road*
	Hills End
Sperry, A.	*The Boy Who Was Afraid*
Townsend, J. R.	*The Intruder*
Wain, J.	*A Message From the Pig-Man* (short story)

Non-fiction Prose

Baker, P.	*Martin Luther King*
Brittain, V.	*Testament of Youth*
Frank, A.	*The Diary of Anne Frank*
Murphy, D.	*Full Tilt*
Southall, I.	*Seventeen Seconds*

Verse

Drayton, M.	*Agincourt*
Hughes, L.	*Mother to Son*
	Still Here
Macaulay, T. B.	*How Horatius Held the Bridge*
Summers, H.	*The Rescue*
Tennyson, A.	*The Charge of the Light Brigade*
Van Doren, M.	*Indomitable*

Further Activities

The most important single extension of this theme is into the area of everyday life: in what ways do the ordinary people around us display courage? The answer is often that they do so in quite secret and unexpected ways. Any kind of research on such a topic has, of course, to be undertaken with sympathy and sensitivity, since the answer will often lie among the least privileged members of society: the old, the poor, those with disabilities. It could begin with a detailed examination of local newspapers, to look for single acts of courage – the child rescued from the canal or burning building – and then move on to these quieter (and, one feels, more common types of courage.)

Contents

THE DAYS OF OUR LIVES

* Pupil's book page
** Teacher's book page

Analysis of activities

Discussion: 15   17   T11   T12   T13   T14
Writing: personal   17   T13
        in role   T11
        verse   T13
        (see also 'Research')
Comprehension: questions   19
             missing sentences   29
Word study: 30
Language study: T14
Research: T11   T12
Drama: game   T15
        role-play   T15

Doodlebugs and evacuation

Pupil's book pages **16–19**   research; discussion; writing

Research

World War II is still 'living history'. That means that you can still find out about it from people living today – friends, relatives, and local people.

Find out as much as you can about what your neighbourhood was like during World War II.

1   **Ask** family, friends, neighbours, teachers, other local people.
2   **Read** any books that your local library may have about the district between 1939 and 1945.
3   **Borrow** (if you can) any books, newspapers, magazines and souvenirs people may have dating back to the war.

Such research is a most useful introduction to literature set in wartime such as *Carrie's War*, *Fireweed*, and *The Machine Gunners* (All listed on the Extensions page at the end of the unit).

Discussion points

1   What do you think it felt like to be an evacuee?
2   How do you think the little girl felt who wrote this letter home?

> Dear Mum I hope you are well. I don't like the man's face. I don't like the lady's face much. Perhaps it will look better in daylight. I like the dog's face best.★

3   Read the extract from *Carrie's War* on page 27. How do you think those children felt.

Writing

You are an evacuee. Write a description of what it was like to leave home, travel to an unknown place and live with people you had never met before.

★**Theo Barker (ed.):** *The Long March of Everyman*

All changed

Pupil's book pages **20–1**

Discussion points
1 What impression have you formed of Charlie?
2 How do you think he felt when he came out of the Underground station?
3 What do you think the building worker thought of him?
4 How well do you think Charlie is going to survive out of prison – and why?

Research
Find out how much the area where you live has changed over the past 25 years.

A *Finding out*
1 If your family has lived in the district for a long time, talk to your parents and other relatives.
2 Talk to any teachers in the school who have lived in the area a long time.
3 Talk to people in your street or estate.
4 Talk to people in local shops.
5 Go to the library and ask for help in the *Reference* section.

B *Reporting*
1 Draw a map to mark the changes that have taken place.
2 Make a list of the main changes that have happened, in order, with dates where possible.
3 Write down people's opinions of these changes – or, if you can, record interviews with them.

Blackberry-picking

Pupil's book page **22**   discussion; writing

Questions to think and talk about

1   How does this poem make you feel?
2   Why does it have that effect on you?
3   Does it remind you of anything that has ever happened to you?
4   Why do you think a grown man chose to write a poem about a subject like this – is it important enough?

Writing

The poem describes a pattern of excitement followed by disappointment. Can you remember any occasions in your own life when you have experienced such a pattern? Describe what happened as a story or a poem.

Seamus Heaney was born in 1939 in County Derry, N. Ireland, and was brought up in the country. Like Langston Hughes he writes of childhood experiences in the country. He lives and works in Belfast.

Aunt Sue's Stories

Pupil's book page **23**   discussion

Questions to think and talk about

1   Who is Aunt Sue?
2   What are her stories about?
3   Where did she get her stories from?
4   Why is the child so attentive?
5   Have you ever been told stories that are not 'out of any book at all' but right out of someone's own life?
6   What is the difference to you between reading stories in a book and being told real life stories by someone who knows about them?
7   Does it make any difference if the person doing the telling is on television?

Langston Hughes was a black American poet (1902–1967). He was born in Missouri and brought up in Kansas, but lived most of his adult life in New York.

Algebra lesson

Pupil's book pages **24–5**

Questions to think and talk about

1   Describe the school that Errol attended.
2   Why was he so interested in the birds?
3   Why does he say 'Me a go lick dem birds . . .'?
4   What explanations does he give for crying so much?
5   How does Ricky react to what happened?
6   Ricky is Errol's friend. What do you think of the way he speaks to Errol?

Language study

Errol has written the conversations in his story in Jamaican *dialect* (or *Creole*), so that they sound as if they are being spoken. At first, to a non-Jamaican, they seem difficult to understand. They differ in three main ways:

Pronunciation   He writes *rang* where some people would say *wrong*.
Vocabulary   He uses special words like *jinnal*
Sentences   He builds up some of his sentences in a different way.
For example Ricky says:
Miss Brown lick you 'ard today, eh?
People from another part of Britain might say
'Ere, vat Miss Brarn giv' you a clout din' she?

Choose a dialect that you know well, and write a short conversation in it.

This piece of work is better done if it is discussed and prepared (by allowing time for thought and observation) before the writing begins. If tape recorders are available, then so much the better. It is, however, very important to stress that dialects are simply different forms of the language – different according to the group whose language they are. The notion that one dialect is necessarily superior to another is illogical, if widespread. How the work is approached depends of course on the ethnic composition of the class. One of the problems that a child from a West Indian family faces is just this matter of dialect. To some extent all regional dialects are generally regarded as inferior (although this is not as widespread as it used to be). West Indian dialects, however, are seen by many people as different in kind from and specifically inferior to any British regional dialect. Yet their dialect – especially in the case of West Indians (who have no other language to use at home) is just as much their natural 'home' language as the dialect of a white child from Newcastle, Liverpool or Glasgow. In multicultural classrooms, therefore, (and in many monocultural ones) the topic needs handling with care and sensitivity if it is not just going to reinforce prejudices that already exist.

Any Saturday in 1920

Pupil's book pages **26–8**   interviewing

Lil Smith's memories should provide a powerful incentive for children to want to talk to grandparents and others of their generation. The easiest way to do this is to suggest that they simply talk and then report the conversation back in speech or writing. If a tape recorder is used, various problems can creep in. Often children (and 'subjects') are embarrassed by the intrusion of the machine and the results are disappointing. Such interviewing is best done by pairs of children after some kind of practice. The following preparatory activities may help.

The question game
Work in pairs. One person asks the other a question. The other answers but must not use the words 'yes' or 'no'. If he does he loses a point.

Example   A: Do you like fishing?
             B: I find it rather boring.

Now it is B's turn to ask a question:

             B: Have you ever visited the Tower of London?
             A: I did once, last year.
                Have you?
             B: I have never had that pleasure, but I have been to Paris. Have you?
             A: No.

Here B wins.

Interviews
The partners decide who is to be the interviewer and who is to be interviewed. The interviewer sets himself to find out some detail about the other person, but doesn't say what it is. He asks a number of questions and at the right moment slips in a question that will require the information he wants. The person interviewed has to stop this happening, but doesn't know what his interviewer is trying to find out. The interviewee must always tell the truth and cannot refuse to answer a question. He can, of course, attempt to lead the interview off in a different direction.

Puzzles

Pupil's book page **29–30**   answers

Evacuees
1 line 16 after '. . . in hers.'
2 line 5 after '. . . "it seems."'
3 line 23 after '. . . taken away.'
4 line 10 after '. . . at school.'
5 line 8 after '. . . do that.'

Extensions

Further Reading

Fiction Prose

Bawden, N.	*Carrie's War*
Burton, H.	*In Spite of All Terror*
Chaplin, S.	*The Leaping Lad and other stories*
Holm, A.	*I Am David*
Naughton, B.	*The Bees Have Stopped Their Working and other stories*
	A Dog Called Nelson
	My Pal Spadger
Richter, H. P.	*Friedrich*
	I Was There
	The Time of the Young Soldiers
Serraillier, I.	*The Silver Sword*
Steinbeck, J.	*The Red Pony*
Thomas, D.	*A Visit to Grandpa's*
Turner, P.	*Dunkirk Summer*
Walsh, J. P.	*Fireweed*
Westall, R.	*The Machine Gunners*

Non-fiction Prose

Brighton Books, published by Macmillan

The English Centre	*Our Lives* – Young People's Autobiographies
Church, R.	*Over the Bridge*
Frank, A.	*The Diary of Anne Frank*
Kirkup, J.	*The Only Child*
Lee, L.	*Cider With Rosie*
Sillitoe, A.	*Raw Material*
Smith, L.	*The Good Old Bad Old Days* (Centreprise)
Thomas, D.	*Quite Early One Morning*
Thomas, L.	*This Time Tomorrow*

Much interesting, vivid material is being produced by the various community publishing ventures that developed during the 1970s. Some of the better known at the time of publication were:

London	Stepney Books c/o 196 Cable Street, London, E.1
	Centreprise 136 Kingsland High Street, London, E.8.
Bristol	Bristol Broadsides Publishing Co-operative 110 Cheltenham Road, Bristol 6
Manchester	The Gate House Project c/o ICI Blackley Works, Waterloo Street, Blackley, Manchester

Further information is available from The Federation of Worker Writers and Community Publishers, at the Centreprise address.

Contents

ALL WINTER LONG

* Pupil's book page
** Teacher's book page

Analysis of activities

Discussion: 31   33   T19   T21   T22
Writing: in role   33
            descriptive   T20
            thought flow   T20
            poetry   T20
            haiku   T20
Comprehension: sequencing   32   T19
                   true/false   35
                   questions   35
                   cloze   43
                   poetry   T20
                   prediction   T22
Research: T19
Drama: playmaking   T21

Illustrations

Pupil's book page **31**   discussion

The countries in which the photographs were taken are: Afghanistan, Norway, Japan.

Indian warning

Pupil's book pages **32–3**   sequencing; research

Sequencing

Correct order: 1 – 4– 5 – 9 – 3 – 8 – 2 – 6 – 7

This technique is normally used in this book as one of the *Puzzles*. It is, however, an interesting and unusual way to begin a theme unit. As has been suggested before, the greatest benefit from such an exercise is gained when it is done in pairs or small groups who discuss the problem before arriving at a solution. In this way individual children are encouraged to make explicit their intuitive responses to meaning and structure.

Research

The Indian's 'Weather Forecast' is based on an old saying for his people. We have many such sayings about the weather, for example:

   Red sky at night, shepherd's delight;
   Red sky at morning, shepherd's warning.
and
   Rain before seven, fine before eleven.

Make a collection of as many of these sayings as you can: parents and grandparents may be able to help you. For each one explain what it means and how useful you think it is likely to be.

Avalanche

Pupil's book pages **34–5**   answers

True or false

1 true	6 true
2 true	7 false
3 false	8 true
4 false	9 false
5 true	10 false

The Warrior of Winter

Pupil's book page **36**

This is likely to prove the most difficult of the poems. Since there are six poems in the unit altogether this is no real disadvantage. It may be used for individual study, or – with classes that the teacher thinks can cope with it – discussed with the class as a whole.

Reading and thinking

You will probably need to read this poem several times before you can really 'get inside it'. As you read it, try to see its pictures in your mind. When you have read it two or three times, start asking yourself these questions:

Who exactly is the warrior – what does he stand for?
What or who is the star?
Why are they fighting against each other?
What does the star want?
What is the warrior trying to defend?
Who wins in the end?

Poems

Pupil's book page **37**

The Mother's Song

When you have read and thought about how the mother feels, think about the father. He built this igloo they are sheltering in. He knows very well what a blizzard can do. What are his thoughts? How does he feel? What does he want?

Write: The Father's Song

Three haiku

The pattern of a haiku is explained on page 184. Write a haiku of your own on some aspect of winter. Choose your own topic, or one of these:

Snowman
Thaw
Snow in the City
Winter Wind

Thaw

This poem literally gives us a bird's eye view of its subject. As you read it, try to see in your mind what the rooks see. Now imagine that you are a rook flying high above fields or city. Describe what you can see.

Fire on Christmas Eve

Pupil's book page **38**

discussion;
playmaking

Discussion
There are five main characters in this story:

the storyteller ('I')

Jim

Jim's mother: Mrs Prothero

Jim's father: Mr Prothero

Jim's aunt: Miss Prothero

They face a serious situation, a fire. They all react in different ways.
What do we learn about what they are like as people?

Playmaking
Groups of 3, 4, or 5.

1 Each choose a different character from the story.
2 Choose one of these titles:
   Stuck in the Lift
   The Burglary
   The Flood
   Miss Prothero is Arrested
3 Discuss what could happen in a play with that title and the characters
   you have chosen. How would each of them behave?
4 Decide where the play happens and when.
5 Decide how it starts, but do not plan the rest of it in too much detail.
6 Try it out.
7 When you have run through the whole play discuss how it went and
   how it could be improved. Ask yourselves these questions:
   a How can we make the story clearer for an audience?
   b How can we make the characters more true to life?
   c Is the ending strong enough, or can we think of a better one?
8 Practise your play again, with any changes you have decided upon.

The drama instructions are, of course, best given orally and one stage at
a time. The exercise could also be used as an exercise in play-writing or
story-writing for individuals.

Alone on the trail

Pupil's book pages **39–42**   discussion

The reading level of this extract is high. Some teachers may prefer to read it to their classes. The extract naturally invites speculation about the man's chances of survival. The questions that follow are intended to encourage and shape that speculation. Discussion of them can well be followed by reading the rest of the story to the class. It is to be found in various current collections of short stories and in *Great Short Works of Jack London* edited by Earle Labor in the paperback *Perennial Classics* series published by Harper & Rowe.

Questions to think and talk about
1 In what ways was the day out of the ordinary?
2 Why was the man optimistic?
3 What were his limitations?
4 What were the dog's feelings?
5 When was the man first surprised by the cold?
6 On what other occasions was he surprised by it?
7 How did he react to this surprise?
8 What mistakes did he make?
9 What chance do you give him of getting to the camp on time?
10 What chance do you give him of surviving at all?

Puzzles

Pupil's book pages $43-4$ answers

The Indian's warning

As was pointed out in the Introduction, this type of exercise is best tackled in pairs or threes. This is because the process of discussion, of sharing meanings of a text (and how one acquires them) is a vital part of the development of comprehension. It should also be re-emphasized that the pupils are not being asked to guess the actual words used in the original, but to work out suitable words to fill the spaces. In some cases there is only one word. In others there are a number of possibilities. In the answers given below, a few possible variants are given in brackets, but there are, of course, others.

1 I
2 for
3 a (any, my)
4 in (cattle)
5 spring (April)
6 Suits
7 feel
8 Pa (he, Royal)
9 head
10 got
11 and (even)
12 to
13 afford (manage)
14 well (nicely)
15 I
16 with (for)
17 for
18 quickly (back, thoughtfully)
19 looked (glanced)
20 was
21 Ma
22 when (as)
23 had
24 in (down)
25 sewing (reading, working)
26 wrong
27 loaves (bread)
28 white (table)
29 Pa (he)
30 tea
31 I
32 thing
33 to (into)
34 got
35 for (then)
36 load (lot)
37 Charles (Gracious)
38 his
39 little (sister)
40 Laura
41 at
42 her (Laura, Carrie, Grace)
43 thing

Word study
1 claims
2 homestead
3 unstable
4 vibration
5 quag
6 blunders
7 shattered
8 quilt
9 speculating
10 undulations

Clouds
Answers   A2   B4   C1   D3

23

Extensions

Further Reading

Fiction Prose

Balderson, M.	*When Jays Fly to Barbmo*
Christopher, J.	*The World in Winter*
Dickens, C.	*The Christmas Books*
	Pickwick Papers
Hildick, E. W.	*Louie's Snowstorm*
London, J.	*To Build a Fire*
	The Call of the Wild
	White Fang
Van der Loeff, A. R̆.	*Avalanche!*
Wilder, L. I.	*The Long Winter*

Non-fiction Prose

Durrell, G.	*My Family and Other Animals*
Lee, L.	*Cider With Rosie*
Thomas, D.	*Quite Early One Morning*
Thompson, F.	*Lark Rise to Candleford*
Uttley, A.	*Country Child*

Verse

Bownas and Thwaite (eds.)	*The Penguin Book of Japanese Verse*
Finnegan, R. (ed.)	*The Penguin Book of Oral Poetry* (for eskimo verse)
Hardy, T.	*Snow in the Suburbs*
Hughes, T.	*Season Songs*
	Moortown
MacNiece, L.	*Snow*
Wilson, R. (ed.)	*Time's Delights*

Further Activities

Group research and work projects can consider the effects of winter on areas different from that in which the class live. If they live in the city they can collect material about the effects of a hard winter on those who make their living in the country, or, for example, in mountainous areas where winter sports are popular.

There appears to be no readily available anthology of winter poetry. A group might set themselves the aim of browsing through available anthologies of poetry and making their own collection of such poetry.

SNOWED UP!

This unit is designed to be used by individuals or small groups. Once the material has been introduced to the class as a whole it is capable of being used by children for long periods without further assistance from the teacher. It is divided into the following sections:

1 Introductory page
2 Beginning
3 The first day: Settling in
4   What's for supper?
5   Bedtime
6 The second day: Next morning
7   Diversions . . .
8   . . . and alarms
9 The third day: Thaw!
10   Letter home
11   The journey
12 Afterwards: Safe at last

Section 1 can be used for preliminary discussion and pooling of ideas. The teacher can also use this opportunity for determining whether the work is to be done individually or in small groups. If the latter, then where the heading *Thinking* appears in the text, this should be taken as a signal for group discussion. The *Writing* sections will still be tackled individually, although groups may decide to share assignments out, when there is a choice.

Section 2 provides the groundwork for the rest of the project and should therefore be done in some detail. If it appears that there is too much here for each individual to tackle everything on the page, then the class can be divided into groups and the work divided up as suggested above.

Section 3 is more straightforward, and it should be possible for individuals to tackle the work involved in one, or at most two, short periods.

Section 4 on the other hand may require some research both into dietary requirements and methods of preparing food. For this reason it is useful, if possible, to give advance warning of this section so that people can make necessary enquiries, whether at home or at school.

Section 5 is less demanding. Those who are put off by the word 'poem' can be instructed to write a series of thoughts, instead, or even a dream-story.

Section 6 The *Thinking* points here are much better discussed than left to individuals. The teacher who is not using small group work may well find it useful to put these questions to the class as a whole, before writing is begun.

Section 7 Some children may need help in the early stages of constructing board games. The basic outline of a dice-and-counters board game can be discussed with them. The simplest is the straightforward race from start to finish – possibly with penalty and reward squares on the way. Children could, perhaps, be asked to bring in a few such games to see how they are planned. If they stick to the simple race pattern and start by roughing out the number of squares and deciding a basic outline, then there should not be too much difficulty. Useful language work can come out of the writing of clear unambiguous rules for these games.

Section 8 is similar to uses of conversation snippets in Section B of the book, and can well be used as an opportunity to revise them, or to introduce them when this project is ended.

Section 9 involves quite a lot of thinking and writing. It is one, therefore, that is quite suitable for division between the members of a group.

Sections 10 and 11 are straightforward.

Section 12 can be used as a simple writing exercise, or the TV interview may initiate a piece of role-play *before* the writing is attempted.

Contents

* Pupil's book page
** Teacher's book page

Analysis of activities

Discussion: 55   57   T29   T31
Writing: narrative   57   T31
         script   T30
         conversation   T32
         in role   T33
Comprehension: 59   T31
Word study: 68
Project: T29
Group work: radio play   T30
           research/discussion   T32
           poetry-reading   T32
Drama: role-play   T33
      radio play   T30

Illustrations

Pupil's book page **55**

Discussion points

1   What questions would you like to ask, in order to understand these drawings better?
2   What would be the *problems* of building houses like these?
3   What would be the *advantages* of building houses – real homes – underground like this?
4   Would you ever choose to live in an underground house? What are your reasons?

Project

Design your own underground house. Before you actually design it, think about the answers to some of these questions:

a   What site would you choose: hilltop, hillside, mountainside, wood-land, cliff face . . . where?
b   How would you fit your house into the landscape? (Notice how Wells has made his house a part of the wood in which it is sited.)
c   What rooms would you have and how would they link together?

When you have thought about these points, do some rough drawings of your house and site. Then:

1   Make a final drawing or drawings, with labels to show what everything is.
2   Write an explanation, saying what your house is like and why.

Manhunt underneath Vienna

Pupil's book pages **56—7**

script writing;
group work

Writing a script

In this story the *sounds* are very important — voices and noises echoing through tunnels underground. Write a radio script about a manhunt underground. Either use this story, or make up one of your own.

There is more information about scriptwriting on page 176.

Group work

Prepare to perform one of the scripts you have written.

1 Read the script through.
2 Discuss and then cast the parts.
3 Each study your own part.
4 Prepare any sound effects you need.
5 Rehearse your play.

REMEMBER: this is a radio play. The audience cannot see anything, except what they imagine as they hear your voices.

This can be completed in a number of different ways:

1 As a taped play, if any recorders are available.
2 Using a microphone and amplifier (preferably with the cast screened from the loudspeaker to avoid both distraction and feedback).
3 As a reading.

Just a hole in the ground

Pupil's book pages **58—9**

discussion

Clearly the *idea* and the drawing can lead to much interesting discussion. The information can also be used to support and/or introduce the extract from *The Third Man*, which it follows.

Escape from a prisoner–of–war camp

Pupil's book pages **60–1**

comprehension;
discussion; writing

Questions

1 Draw a diagram with labels to show the pattern of the shafts and tunnels.
2 Why did the tunnellers wear hats?
3 How did the air pump work?
4 Why were there two tunnels?
5 How did they get rid of the clay they dug out?
6 What feelings did Peter have during and after tunnelling?

Discussion points

Eric Williams writes: 'It is an extraordinary truth that tunnels, the most popular means of getting out of a prison camp, were not often successful. Beneath Stalag-Luft III, the 'escape-proof' camp . . . over 100 tunnels were dug. Yet . . . only six tunnellers were lucky enough to get clean away.'
Eric Williams, *Great Escape Stories*

1 Why do you think tunnels were so popular?
2 Why weren't they more successful?
3 Knowing this, if you were a prisoner of war, would you have tried to escape by tunnelling?

Writing

Write a story about either

a an attempt to escape from imprisonment
b some other escape
c being trapped underground

Coal miner

Pupil's book pages **62–3**   group discussion

Group work

1   Study the picture and the piece of writing. From them make a list of the special qualities and skills required by a miner. Add to your list any points that are not in the book, but which you know about from elsewhere.
2   Make similar lists for these jobs:

dustman   hospital nurse   lorry-driver

3   Compare the two lists and answer these two questions:
   a   Which of the jobs would you prefer to do (put them in order of preference)?
   b   Which job is best paid?

This could, of course, be organized as individual work followed by class discussion.

A Collier's Wife

Pupil's book pages **63–4**   reading aloud; writing

Group work

Prepare a group reading of the poem.

1   Read it through carefully, alone.
2   Discuss it, working out together what the difficult words mean.
3   Work out which character says which lines.
4   Cast the parts.
5   Practise reading the poem as a conversation.

Writing

Write a conversation or a conversation-poem about one of the following:

a   the door-to-door salesman
b   bad news
c   the gossip
d   the street accident

A Collier's Wife

role-play

Role-play

A series of short conversations for two people. They can all be done in the same pairs, or partners can be changed after each one. In each conversation the basic roles are the same:

A: housewife or husband at home alone
B: someone who calls at the front door

Conversation 1
B is a neighbour who has come to borrow something. (B – decide what: A – decide how you feel about this neighbour.)

Conversation 2
B is a neighbour with a particularly juicy piece of gossip she has just heard (B – decide what). A is very busy. (A – decide why.)

Conversation 3
B is a door-to-door salesman. (B – decide what you are selling.) A is not very interested.

Variations on Conversation 3
i   For some reason A is very nervous about strangers.
ii A is so bored that she/he wants to have a good chat – without, of course, wanting to buy anything.

Conversation 4
It is General Election time. B is the local Conservative candidate. A's family have always voted Labour.

Conversation 5
A is worried because his/her son/daughter is an hour late home from school. B knows why (B – decide what has happened) and comes across, as a neighbour, to tell A.

Conversation 6
B is a police officer. (B – decide why you are calling on A.) A is embarrassed by the arrival of the police. (A – decide why and what you do about it.)

Orpheus & Eurydice

Pupil's book pages **65–6**   writing

Writing

The story is told from Orpheus' point of view. Try to imagine what it
was like for Eurydice. When she died, she was taken from the world she
loved into the dark regions of Hades – all alone, not knowing where
she was going or what would happen to her. Tell *her* story in your own
words. Describe how she felt and what happened when Orpheus tried
to rescue her.

Extensions

Further Reading

Fiction Prose

Adams, R.	*Watership Down*
Aiken, J.	*The Whispering Mountain*
Briggs, R.	*Fungus the Bogeyman*
Carter, B.	*The Perilous Descent*
Church, R.	*The Cave*
Faulkner, J. M.	*Moonfleet*
Grahame, K.	*The Wind in the Willows*
Household, G.	*Rogue Male*
King, C.	*Stig of the Dump*
Lawrence, D. H.	*An Odour of Chrysanthemums*
Macdonald, G.	*The Princess and the Goblin*
	The Princess and Curdie
Tolkien, J. R. R.	*The Hobbit* (beautifully read on an Argo record by Nicol Williamson)
Twain, M.	*The Adventures of Tom Sawyer*
Verne, J.	*Journey to the Centre of the Earth*

Non-fiction Prose

Macaulay, D.	*Underground*
Williams, E.	*The Wooden Horse*

Further Activities

Areas of exploration: the development of underground railways
potholing
'underground' political movements, the resistance.

Contents

POSSIBLE FUTURES

* Pupil's book page
** Teacher's book page

Analysis of activities

Discussion: 69   71   T37   T39   T40
Writing: newspaper report   69   71
            in role   71
            story   T39 T40
            poem   T42
Comprehension: questions   73
                true/false   73
                sequencing   79
Word study: T37
Language study: T39
Drama: developing a group situation   T38
Group project: T41

Illustrations

Pupil's book page **69**   discussion

The illustrations and question on this page can be used at the beginning of work on the theme, or, alternatively, towards the end, perhaps when class or groups are working on the project relating to *Next?*.

Martians

Pupil's book pages **70–1**   word study

Each of these words occurs in the story.

List A	*List B*	*List C*	*List D*
impact	curate	tranquil	pulverized
beam	motionless	adjacent	tympanic
tentacles	rampart	verge	anatomically
hunched	suburban	denser	terrestrial
ruddy	dispersed	endeavouring	consequence

1 Work on one list at a time.
2 Find each word in the list in the story.
3 Write each word and against it write what you think it means.
4 If you are not sure – have a guess based on the sentence it is in.
5 When you have done all five words, look them *all* up in the dictionary.
6 Write down the meanings of any that you got wrong.

The lists are progressively more difficult, of course, and for many classes List D can more easily be used as a straight dictionary exercise.

Space colonies

Pupil's book pages **72–3** drama

What follows provides only the bare bones of a lesson or series of lessons based on the idea of a spaceship travelling to the stars. It concentrates on the point that those initiating the journey would be committing unborn generations to live and die on the journey. It suggests one way in which simple pair conversations can be developed into a full scale confrontation between the parents and the children whom they have just informed of the facts of their situation.

Pair conversations

Decide who is A and who is B. Change round after each conversation.

1   A – NASA scientist   B – reporter
    NASA is holding a news conference to explain its plans for a space colony. A is the spokesman. B is very doubtful about the whole thing – particularly the expense involved.

2   A – NASA scientist   B – a member of A's family (wife/husband/son/daughter).
    A has been offered the chance to go on the first space journey to the stars. A tells B about the chance and what it involves. Of course the whole family will have to come. They will never reach the stars themselves, but their children's children's children's children will . . .

3   A – parent   B – child
    The journey to the stars has been going on for just over a hundred years. A was born on board the spaceship as was, of course, B. Now B is old enough to be told about the journey, about earth – and about the fact that B will die before the journey is completed.

Group scenes

1   A group of parents have just told their children about the journey. They discuss how the children received the news.
2   A group of children have just been told about the journey. They talk about their reactions.
3   Children and parents confront each other. The children tell the parents what they think about their situation.

Poems

Pupil's book pages **74–5**

Bleep

Writing

Suppose other machines took it into their own minds to do what they liked. Write a poem or a story about a machine that stops doing as it is told and goes off on its own. Choose your own machine, or one from this list.

hedge trimmer
washing machine
lawnmower
vacuum cleaner
electric drill
food mixer

First Men on Mercury

Questions to think and talk about

1   What is the attitude of the men when they arrive on Mercury and meet its inhabitants?
2   How do the Mercurians react to them?
3   What happens to the men?
4   Why does it happen?
5   Has this poem a 'message'? Or is it just a bit of fun? Or what is it?

Language study

1   Make up meanings for the Mercurian's language. Write down what *Bawr stretter* and the other things they say mean.
2   Invent some other words and expressions in Mercurian.
3   Write a conversation between two Mercurians.

Writing

The first men to land on Mercury return to earth. Tell the story of what happens when they get back.

QT-1

Pupil's book page **76**   discussion

Questions to think and talk about
1 In what ways is QT-1 different from other robots?
2 What does QT-1 think it sees out of the space window?
3 Why does it think this?
4 What is QT-1's opinion of the human body?
5 What does QT-1 think of Powell's explanation of space?
6 QT-1 says, 'It is obvious that no being can create another that is superior to the maker.' Who does it think is superior: Powell or itself?
7 Therefore, who does QT-1 think made whom?
8 If so, what might happen next in this story, do you think?
9 Do you think such a situation could ever arise in real life?
10 Are there any ways in which machines already 'run' our lives?

An ape about the house

Pupil's book page **77**   discussion;
                                                               writing

Questions to think and talk about
Suppose that in the future it was possible to breed a 'superchimp' like Dorcas. Men would have slaves to do all the boring jobs for them.
1 Would it be right to do this?
2 Would it be wise?
3 Might it go wrong?
4 Should present experiments in biological engineering be continued?

Writing
This extract comes from the very beginning of a story. Think of what might happen in the story: how do the children, the parents, and Granny react to Dorcas? How do they treat her? How do they speak to her? What do they get her to do? How does she behave?

When you have thought about these points, write the rest of the story as you think it ought to be.

Then . . . now . . . next?

Group work

A Discussion points

What is the future likely to offer?

1 What forms of transport will be available in the year 2050?
2 What kind of housing will people have then?
3 How will they communicate with each other?
4 Will life be better as a result of such developments?

B Project

1 Produce a folder of materials, or a wallchart showing what life will be like in the year 2050.
2 Choose one topic each to concentrate on. Select your own, or take one from this list.

housing education transport communications clothing
food sport entertainment farming crime and the police

3 Include a variety of different types of material in the project as a whole. Some possibilities are:

writing: stories, factual accounts, interviews, poems; drawings, maps, charts, diagrams, statistics, cuttings.

Puzzles

Dorcas
The correct order is: $2 - 6 - 4 - 1 - 5 - 3 - 7$

The solar system
1 – D
2 – G
3 – A
4 – F
5 – B
6 – H
7 – E
8 – C

Extensions

Further Reading

Fiction Prose

Asimov, I.	*The Martian Way*
	I, Robot (and others)
Blish, J.	*The Star Dwellers*
Boulle, P.	*Monkey Planet*
Bradley, R.	*The Silver Locusts*
	The Illustrated Man (and others)
Chambers, R.	*The Ice Warrior*
Christopher, J.	*The Guardians*
	The Lotus Caves
	The Tripods Trilogy (and others)
Clarke, A. C.	*Of Time and Stars*
	2001 (and others)
Crichton, M.	*The Andromeda Strain*
	The Terminal Man
Crispin, E.	*Best SF* (a series)
Dickinson, P.	*The Changes* sequence
Fisk, N.	*Trillions*
	Space Hostages (and others)
Heinlein, R.	*Orphans of the Sky*
	The Red Planet (and others)
Lewis, C. S.	*Out of the Silent Planet*
	Perelandra
	That Hideous Strength
Neale, N.	*Quatermass* (in its various manifestations)
Norton, A.	*Catseye* (and others)
Orwell, G.	*1984*
Sheckley, R.	*The Robert Sheckley Omnibus*
Spielberg, S.	*Close Encounters of the Third Kind*
Verne, J.	*20,000 Leagues Under the Sea*
	Journey to the Centre of the Earth
Wells, H. G.	*War of the Worlds*
	First Men on the Moon
	The Time Machine
Wyndham, J.	*Day of the Triffids*
	The Midwich Cuckoos
	The Chrysalids

Contents

* Pupil's book page
**Teacher's book page

THE HORROR ... THE **HORROR!**

43

Analysis of activities

Discussion: 81   83   T46   T47

Writing: personal   83
               radio script   T45
               opinion   85
               newspaper report   T45
               narrative   T46
               descriptive   T46

Comprehension: questions   85
                     drawing   T46
                     word replacement   93

Word study: 94   T46

Drama: radio play   T45
             role-play   T45
             playmaking   T46

Group work: T45   T46

Terror in the night

Pupil's book pages **82–3**   writing;
group work/drama

Writing
Write a radio script based on the story. There are instructions on how to do this on page 176. Try to do it without using a storyteller. You will probably find that you have to write extra things for Carrie and Nick to say. You will certainly need to describe the sound effects.

Group work
Groups of 2, 3, or 4.
1 Choose one of the scripts you have written.
2 Decide who will act each part and who will do the sound effects.
3 Practise the script.
4 Make up and practise the sound effects.
5 Perform or record your scene.

The Amityville horror

Pupil's book pages **84–5**   drama;
writing

Drama: group work
Groups of 4 or 5.

1	Cast the parts:	2 members of the Lutz family; 2 or 3 reporters.
2	LUTZ FAMILY:	Read the passage through again. Decide whether your story is true or a fake. Make sure that you can remember all the details of it. Don't talk to the reporters about it yet.
3	REPORTERS:	You are going to interview the Lutz family about their experiences. Decide whether you think that this sort of thing is credible or not. Don't talk to them yet.
4	PREPARATION:	Arrange some chairs and a table so that you can have the interview.
5	THE INTERVIEW:	It is the day after the Lutz family have fled from their house. They have had little or no sleep. Reporters have finally persuaded them to be interviewed about what happened to them.
6	STARTING:	Sit in the right places; think about what you are going to say first. When you are all ready, begin the scene.

Writing
Write the newspaper report that is printed as a result of the interview.

The thing   Prince Kano   A Meeting

Pupil's book pages **86–7**   discussion; comprehension; writing; drama

Questions to think and talk about
1   Do you find any of these three pieces of writing 'scary'?
2   If so, which? And why?
3   If not, what kind of story do you find frightening?
4   Why are they frightening?
5   Are written stories more frightening than TV films, or less frightening?

The thing: comprehension (drawing)
Draw a picture of the Thing.

The thing: writing
Write a story about the Thing.

Prince Kano: writing
Write the story of what happens next.

A Meeting: group drama
Groups of 4 or 5.
After this strange meeting, George 1 (or George 2) returns to his family. He is then haunted by George 2 (or George 1). Make up a group play based on this situation.

A guide to horrorland

Pupil's book pages **88–9**   writing; word study

Word study
1   This is a list of some words that might be used to describe a monster in a horror story:
    fanged   slimy   cadaverous   talons   scales   horrendous luminous   bloodshot   slithering   obese   putrid
2   Make sure that you know what each of these means.
3   Add at least five more words that could be used when writing about a horrifying monster.

Writing
Write a description of a monster using some of the words from your lists.

46

The wish

Pupil's book pages **90–2**   discussion

The best way to present this story is probably to read it to the class, without their following it in their books. In this way the listeners' imaginations can work 'in tune' with that of the boy, as the writer develops the story. With a class one knows well, one can then begin to consider just how real imagined fears can become. With other classes another way in to the discussion is simply to ask why the story is entitled 'The Wish'. This can lead on to a consideration of the extent to which some (all?) people need to be frightened periodically, even if the fears are imaginary. But then what is the difference between an 'imaginary' fear and a 'real' one?

Puzzles

Pupil's book pages **93–4**   answers

Safety
The wrong words, with the original words that they replaced:

noses/safety	telephone/hands
rabbit/fire	raindrops/plates
purple/hungry	drill/lamp
athletic/lonely	hutch/book
shouting/open	shops/door
fry/shut	pickled/said
paddling/smiling	admired/chased
suitcase/dress	international/white
subtract/know	

Jumbled words
Dracula (3)
Ghoul (4)
Medium (5)
Poltergeist (6)
Haunt (1)
Vampire (2)

Extensions

Further Reading
Fiction Prose

Bawden, N.	*Carrie's War*
Bradbury, R.	*Golden Apples of the Sun*
Cooper, S.	*Over Sea Under Stone*
	The Dark is Rising
	Greenwitch
	The Grey King
	Silver on the Tree
	Dawn of Fear
Dahl, R.	*Tales of the Unexpected*
	More Tales of the Unexpected
	Someone Like You
Garner, A.	*Elidor*
	The Owl Service
Haining, P.	*The Ghost's Companion*
Hughes, T.	*The Iron Man*
Le Guin, U.	*A Wizard of Earthsea*
	The Tombs of Atuan
	The Farthest Shore
Lewis, C. S.	*Out of the Silent Planet*
	Perelandra
	That Hideous Strength
Lively, P.	*The Ghost of Thomas Kempe*
Matthews, L. J.	*Super Book of Ghost Stories*
Mayne, W.	*Earthfasts*
Poe, E. A.	*The Tell-Tale Heart*
Shelley, M.	*Frankenstein*
Stoker, B.	*Dracula*

Fontana books of Great Ghost Stories

Non-fiction Prose

Dinsdale, T.	*The Loch Ness Monster*
Hitchcock, A.	*Monster Museum*

Verse

Causley, C. (ed.)	*The Puffin Book of Magic Verse*
Hughes, T.	*The Earth Owl and Other Moon People*
Reeves, J.	*Prefabulous Animiles*
Saunders, D. (ed.)	*Hist Whist*

Further Activities – Research

Questions 5 and 6 on page 81 of the pupil's book can be extended into a full-scale survey of people's attitudes to horror in stories and films. Groups of children can devise questionnaires which they then use on friends and families. This can be extended to cover real things which people find frightening or terrifying – bats, spiders, mice and so on.

This unit, like *Snowed Up!* and *School 2025*, is designed for use by individuals or groups with minimal intervention from the teacher. On the other hand if it is done by individuals, then certain classes will need some assistance with the third and fourth sections, because of the amount of detail involved.

The unit is divided into six sections.

The voyage begins; People and places

Each of these is relatively straightforward. In each the reader is provided with certain data. He is given some guidelines about how to consider this data and then a straightforward writing assignment based on it. The *Thinking* section is important, if the writing is to be successful. It can form the basis of group discussion or, if the project is to be tackled on an individual basis, the teacher may find it useful to have a class discussion based on it, after the class have had a period of individual thought.

The explosion; Tracy!

These two sections are more complex and the teacher will probably find it necessary to check after the *Thinking* stage, that pupils are confident about the detailed information they need to have mastered if they are to write successfully. This mastery is dependent on the ability to understand the plan (and the fact that the vertical part of the route is to be achieved by the use of stairs or lifts, not shown, and not by rock climbing or levitation!)

Abandon ship!

This section contains a considerable amount of thinking but the information to be mastered is not so complex, so major problems should not arise.

Celebrities

This is a shorter section and much more simply constructed than the others.

Timing

Each section may be expected to take up between one and two hours' work, depending on the amount of discussion that takes place.

Drama

The data, illustrations and diagrams could, of course, be used as the basis of a drama project, with or without any of the writing assignments offered.

Contents

* Pupil's book page
** Teacher's book page

Analysis of activities

Discussion: 107   109   T52   T53   T55   T56   T57
Writing: dialogue   109
technical   111
imaginative/personal   T54
from 'inside' a poem   T55
in role   T55
newspaper   T56
advertising copy   111
Comprehension: cloze   120
Word study: 121
Language in use: 120   T53   T54
Drama: role-play   T55
Problem–solving: T57
Project: 111
Group activity: T57

Illustrations

Discussion

1 In what different ways can you remember seeing wheels used today?
2 Some uses of the wheel are becoming outdated. Is this true of any of the wheels illustrated on this page?
3 Can you think of any other uses of the wheel that either are obsolete or soon will be?
4 People are also finding new uses for the wheel. Audio cassettes, for example contain a number of wheels. Can you think of any other recent new uses for the wheel?

Problem

Here are some unusual wheel shapes. Look at them carefully and imagine a different machine in which each of them might be used:

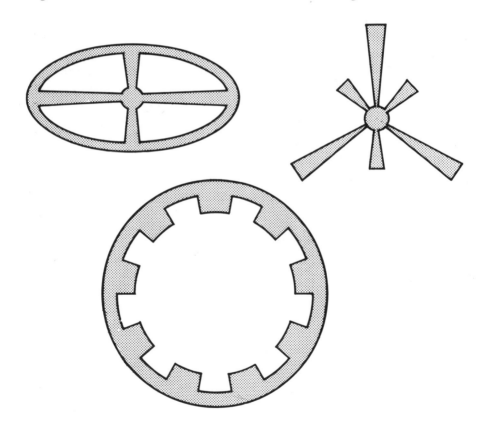

Draw a diagram of each of your three machines and explain
a how it works
b how it makes use of the special wheel it contains.

The bicycle revolution

discussion;
language in use

The discussion of questions 3, 4, 5 can be widened into a more general consideration of sex roles. Is it true to say, for example, that whenever a new development has occurred, men have always wanted to monopolize it and exclude women? Was the question of mobility particularly important and if so, why? (And why bicycles in particular?) Where do these battles take place now? What is the next important battleground for the upholders of women's rights? Such a discussion may well produce predictably stereotyped responses from some of the boys. If so, a more detailed examination of the behaviour of men described in the Flora Thompson extract may prove useful.

Group work: fashionable slang

1   Read the description of the young men's cycling trips. They used a lot of fashionable slang. What would people think of anyone who spoke like that nowadays?

2   What are the present fashionable slang words for these?

scrumptious
awfully good
bally awful
cigarettes
bicycle

3   What other slang words are fashionable at the moment?

4   What is the difference between slang and swearing?

5   When is it all right   to   use slang?
         not all right   swear?

Advertising . . . a bike for every purpose

The language of advertising

1 Read the descriptions of these three bikes:

Commando Star
Stowaway
Shopper

2 Compare the three descriptions for each of these:
   a the amount of *technical information* it contains
   b how much time it spends describing *what the bike looks like*
   c how much it describes *how you can use* the bike

3 Read each one again and ask yourself the question:
   'How much does it expect me to know about bikes already?'

4 Now explain what kind of person each was written for and why.

This is a much more detailed language in use exercise than the one in the pupil's book. It is a difficult exercise if individuals are left to work through it on their own. It can, however, be used with the class as a whole, taking them through questions 1–3 orally, before asking them to write an answer to question 4.

Cycling Down the Street

Writing

What does it feel like to run; or ride a bike really fast; or swing very high; or dive from the top board; or go on the big wheel at the fair?
Describe the thoughts and feelings of a person who is:

   running
or diving from the top board
or on the swing
or cycling downhill
or on the big wheel

Southbound on the Freeway

Pupil's book page **113**

Discussion
What is this poem about?

Writing
The tourist from Orbitville looks first not at a Freeway, but at *one* of the following:

a supermarket
a school
a hospital
a prison
a children's playground

Choose one of them and write his description of human beings based on it. Begin with the line:

The creatures of this star . . .

Write in verse or prose.

Role-play
Eventually the Orbitville tourist meets and communicates with human beings. (Of course he speaks perfect English!) He finds everything about their planets and their lives on it strange and difficult to understand. So they find it difficult to explain things to him. Explore this problem in these pair conversations:

1   A: Orbitville tourist   B: yourself.
    B tries to explain to A what a school is and how it works.
2   As 1, but B is a headteacher.
3   A: Orbitville tourist   B: policeman.
    B explains to A what his job is and why it is necessary.
4   A: Orbitville tourist   B: girl at supermarket checkout.
    B explains to A what a supermarket is, how people use it and what her job is.
5   A: Orbitville tourist   B: leader of trade union that is out on strike.
    B explains to A about unions and strikes.

Nurburgring 1976

Pupil's book pages **114—15**

The pictures: writing

Study the pictures carefully. Use them to help you imagine what it was like to be at the race and to see the crash happen. Write an eye-witness account of it: describe not only how it happened, but also your thoughts and feelings about what you have seen.

Niki Lauda: questions to think and talk about

1 How does Niki Lauda feel about his face?
2 Why was his recovery so remarkable?
3 What was his explanation for going back to racing so quickly?
4 What is your opinion of his decision to return to racing?
5 What impression do you get of Niki Lauda as a person?

Catching a train in Russia

Pupil's book pages **116—17**

comprehension

Questions

1 What was it like on the platform?
2 Why wouldn't the man on the platform let the passengers onto the train?
3 How did this affect the American woman?
4 How did Paul Theroux feel about his compartment?
5 He lists several things that show how luxurious it was – name three of them.
6 What towns would the train go through on the way to Moscow?
7 How would you feel about travelling 6,000 miles on such a train?

What next?

Pupil's book page **118**   group discussion

Discussion points

1 Do you agree with Richard Ballantine that 'eventually motor vehicles have to go'? If so, what will replace them? If not, why do you disagree?

2 What is your reaction to the figures and opinions expressed by Patrick Rivers?

3 What is your reaction to the *Road Accident Figures for 1977*?

4 At what age is a person most likely to be killed or seriously injured in a road accident? Why do you think this is? What should be done about it?

5 The cost of road accidents is at present largely paid by the National Health Service and the Police Service. There are also heavy additional costs for employers. None of this is normally paid for by those involved – at least not directly. Is this fair? Should it be changed? Why should a careful person have to pay more taxes because other people have accidents?

6 What would you do to make the roads safer?

7 What do you expect will be the normal method of travel in this country, for short journeys, by the time you are 40 years old?

8 Here is an example of the kind of problem faced by traffic planners. It concerns an accident black spot. On the map, each black circle marks the site of one serious or fatal accident. How would you solve the problem?

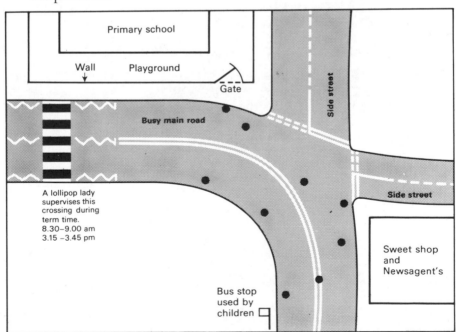

Puzzles

Technical terms

1	D	6	M	11	C	16	H
2	Q	7	F	12	J	17	L
3	E	8	P	13	O		
4	N	9	B	14	G		
5	A	10	I	15	K		

Irish stakes

As was pointed out in the Introduction, this type of exercise is best tackled in pairs or threes. This is because the process of discussion, of sharing meanings of a text (and how one acquires them) is a vital part of the development of comprehension. It should also be re-emphasized that the pupils are not being asked to guess the actual words used in the original, but to work out suitable words to fill the spaces. In some cases there is only one word. In others there are a number of possibilities. In the answers below the original words are given, with a few possible variants in brackets.

1 sports (new, powerful)
2 Ireland
3 traffic
4 to
5 enough
6 Day
7 fast
8 end
9 down
10 eighty
11 the
12 Suddenly (Meanwhile)
13 farmers (men)
14 a (the)
15 was
16 stop
17 drove
18 the
19 ditch
20 field
21 his (the)
22 muddy (wet, swampy)
23 the
24 the
25 tractor
26 the
27 verge
28 went (raced, drove)
29 clappers
30 Irishmen (farmers)
31 until
32 dust
33 to
34 see
35 I
36 Dangerous
37 just
38 time

Extensions

Further Reading

Fiction Prose

Carter, B.	*Four Wheel Drift*
	Speed Six
Chambers, A.	*Cycle Smash*
Cleary, B.	*Runaway Ralph*
De Jong, M.	*Wheel on the School*
Dickinson, P.	*The Changes*
Garfield, L.	*The Sound of Coaches*
Hodges, C. W.	*The Overland Launch*
Martell, G.	*Hit and Run*
Martin, D.	*The Cabby's Daughter*
Merrill, J.	*The Pushcart War*
Naughton, B.	*Spit Nolan* (from *The Goalkeeper's Revenge*)
	Late Night on Watling Street
Nesbit, E.	*The Railway Children*
Stewart, A. C.	*The Quarry Line Mystery*

Non-fiction Prose

Alderson, J.	*Bicycles*
Ballantine, R.	*Richard's Bicycle Book*
Hill, G.	*Bikes*
Kerrod, R.	*Motor Cycles*
Thompson, F.	*Lark Rise to Candleford*
Wise, D. B.	*The Illustrated Encyclopedia of Automobiles*

Verse

Auden, W. H.	*Night Mail*
Levertov, D.	*Merrit Parkway*
MacNeice, L.	*The Cyclist, The Wiper*
Owen, G.	*Salford Road* (collection of poems)
Paterson, A. B.	*Mulga Bill's Bicycle*
Scriven, R. C.	*Wheelwright*
Spender, S.	*The Express*
Stevenson, R. L.	*From a Railway Carriage*
Shapiro, K.	*Cars are wicked, poets think*

Further Activities

The theme lends itself to a variety of follow-up research:

A history of the wheel and its applications

Designing an economic, ecological family car

Further discussion and thought about bicycle safety

An examination of the road safety record of the area around the school and how it could be improved

Local train services: who uses them for what purposes and how they could be improved

Contents

* Pupil's book page
** Teacher's book page

Analysis of activities

Discussion: 121   123   T62   T63   T65
Writing: narrative   T62
   dialogue   T62
   response to literature   T65
Comprehension: questions   125
   sequencing   131
Word study: 132
Language in use: newspapers   T63
Group activities: T63   T64
Drama: T64

Illustrations

Pupil's book page **121**   discussion

Fairly early in the discussion it will probably be necessary to make a distinction between conflict and aggression. Both elements are often present together in a situation and conflicts are often the scenes of aggression, and may be caused by one person's aggressive attitude, but they are clearly distinct.

Pupils should be encouraged to see the wide variety of possible conflicts and the place of conflict in their own lives.

Scrap

Pupil's book pages **122–3**   discussion; writing

Discussion
The key sentence in any discussion of this passage is probably the last one: 'It was enough.' *What* was 'enough'? And 'enough' for *what*? Concepts such as 'honour', 'loss of face' may well arise here, and even the difficult question of whether there are occasions when a person should be prepared to appear dishonourable or a coward because of some more important principle.

Writing
1 Tell the story of what happens next time Gus and Joby meet.
2 The cinema attendant and the middle-aged woman meet in the street and talk about the way Gus and Joby have behaved. Write their conversation.
3 Write a story about someone like you who has to fight – not necessarily a physical fight – against someone older and bigger.

Father and son

Pupil's book pages **124–5**

Group discussion

1 In what ways does the discipline of Theobald's family differ from the discipline of your families?
2 Is it necessary to have *rules* in a family?
3 Is it necessary to have a 'head of the family'?
4 If not, how should conflicts inside a family be sorted out?
5 'All the trouble with young people today is the fault of their parents – they aren't strict enough.' What do you think?

The Way of All Flesh was first published in 1903.

NUC/NAP

Pupil's book page **126**

Writing

1 The NUC strike starts. NUC and NAP make statements to press and TV. The Government gets involved. Things get worse. Make up the front page of a national paper at the height of the strike. Some of the things you could include are:

big headlines
the latest news across the country
interviews with the leaders of NUC and NAP
statements by the Prime Minister and other politicians
comments by the editor
letters from readers.

2 Make up a similar front page but for one of the following events:

rioting breaks out at the national conkers championship
headmasters go on strike (decide why)

This work can well be done by groups rather than individuals. It is particularly effective if large enough sheets of paper (eg. shelving or lining paper) are available to make the thing look realistic. It also benefits, naturally, from study of the make-up of real national papers.

Get off this estate

Pair situations

These situations are for two people, A and B. Before you start, decide who is A and who is B.

1   A is a new boy or girl at the school.
    B is someone of the same age who has always attended that school.

    When A arrives at school on the first day (early) the headmaster tells him to go to the classroom and sit at the desk 'by the window'. He does this. When B comes in he finds A sitting at his desk. He is very annoyed.

2   Same characters.

    Six months ago B found an expensive pen in the street. He took it to the police station. They said that if no one had claimed it after six months he could have it. That has now happened and he uses it at school. When A arrives at the school he sees B using the pen and demands to have it back, saying that he lost it in the street six months ago.

Pair snippets

These are short snippets of conversation. For each one:

1   Read it and think about it.
2   Discuss with your partner who the people might be, and what they might be talking about. Also decide when and where the conversation takes place.
3   Act the conversation and try to include the actual words of the snippet (but don't worry too much if you can't remember them.)

i   A: I don't have to do what you say.
    B: Oh yes you do.
    A: Why should I?

ii A: I saw it first.
    B: No you didn't.
    A: Yes I did. You were nowhere near it.

Group work

In groups of 3, 4, or 5 make up a scene that contains this snippet:

A: Get off this estate.
B: What for?
C: Because it's ours.

Brooklyn Cop
Pupil's book page **127**   discussion

Questions to think and talk about
1 What impression do you get of what the cop looks like?
2 What do lines 6 and 7 mean?
3 A cliché is a word or group of words that has been used so much that it has lost any real meaning. Why is 'Hiya honey' *not* a cliché to the cop?
4 Do you think the writer is on the cop's side?
5 What do the last two lines mean?
6 What do you think Norman MacCaig is saying about the job and life of a cop?

Hunter and hunted
Pupil's book pages **128–30**   writing

Writing
1 Read the story once.
2 Write down your first reactions to it – how you felt and what you thought while you were reading and when you had finished.
3 Read the story again.
4 Add anything you can to what you wrote before. These questions may help you.
   a Did you get clear pictures in your mind of what was happening?
   b Were any of them particularly clear?
   c Does the story contain any surprises? If so, what are they? What effect did they have on you?
   d Why do you think the author wrote the story? What effect do you think he wanted to have on the reader? Was he successful?
   e Do you think it is a good story?

Puzzles

The killing of Grendel
The correct order is: 5 – 2 – 4 – 6 – 8 – 3 – 7 – 1.

Definitions
The words are:

1 innocence
2 tension
3 smouldering
4 onslaught
5 tactics
6 promptly
7 resolution
8 preposterously
9 shirked
10 tissue

Anagrams
The names are:

1 Joby
2 Ernest
3 Roy Fuller
4 D'Arcy Niland
5 Phoebe
6 Carl Sandburg

Extensions

Further Reading

Fiction Prose

Ashley, B.	*Terry on the Fence*
	All My Men
Barstow, S.	*Joby*
Bawden, N.	*A Handful of Thieves*
Byars, B.	*The Eighteenth Emergency*
Crane, S.	*The Red Badge of Courage*
Golding, W.	*Lord of the Flies*
Hinton, S. E.	*The Outsiders*
Lee, L.	*Cider With Rosie*
Line, D.	*Run for Your Life*
Lingard, J.	*The Twelfth Day of July*
Maddock, R.	*The Pit*
Naughton, B.	*Late Night on Watling Street*
Needle, J.	*My Mate Shofig*
Orwell, G.	*Animal Farm*
Richter, H. P.	*Friedrich*
	I Was There
	The Time of the Young Soldiers
Schaefer, J.	*Shane*
Serraillier, I.	*The Silver Sword*
Townsend, J. R.	*The Intruder*
	Hell's Edge
Treece, G.	*Legions of the Eagle*
Westall, R.	*The Machine Gunners*

Verse

Baldwin, M. (ed.)	*Billy The Kid*
Serraillier, I.	*Beowulf the Warrior*

Further Activities

How such a unit proceeds depends very much upon how the class responds to it, both as a group and individually. The material presented in the unit covers a wide range of situations involving both public and personal conflict. It is therefore very much a matter of the teacher observing just where further thought and imagination are called for and developing that aspect of the theme.

Contents

Animals and Man

* Pupil's book page
** Teacher's book page

Analysis of activities

Discussion: 133   135   T71   T72   T73   T74
Writing: personal   135
         variety of approach   T72
         narrative   T72
         fantasy   T73
Comprehension: 136   137   146
Summarizing: T50
Word study: T70
Language in use: register   T72
                 euphemism   T73
Group work: T71   T73
Research: T71
Drama: role-play   T71

Catching an octopus

Pupil's book pages **134–5**

Summary writing

1 Read again the first section of the story (down to the sentence 'It dies on the instant.')
3 Make a list of the main stages in catching and killing an octopus.
3 Use your list to help you write a short description of the octopus hunt. Try not to write more than 80 words.

Word study

List A	List B	List C
cranny	annexed	pellucid
lure	limpid	herculean
decoy	pinioned	tumour
impulse	trance	nausea

1 Find each word in the passage.
2 Write each one on a new line, and against it write what you think it means.
3 If you do not know a word, have a guess based on the sentence it is in.
4 Look *all* the words up in the dictionary.
5 Write the correct meanings of any that you got wrong.

The three lists are in ascending order of difficulty.

Crooks who net the big money

Pupil's book pages **136—7**

group discussion;
research; role play

Group discussion
1 Read the extract from the *Daily Mirror* and discuss it.
2 How can this trade in endangered species be stopped? Work out a plan for stopping it.
3 Report your views to the rest of the class.

This work can serve as an alternative comprehension activity to the questions in the pupil's book, since the discussion cannot be undertaken without thinking about the meaning of the text. In many cases this type of group activity leads to a deeper and more detailed understanding than conventional question-and-answer work.

Research
1 Make a list of world–endangered species. Choose one and find out as much about it as you can. Prepare a short talk about it to give to the rest of the class.
2 Make a list of British mammals. Choose one and find out as much about it as you can. Find out in what ways its existence is threatened by the activities of man. Prepare a short talk about it to give to the rest of the class.
3 Find out the nearest safari park to your school. Find out which animals they have there and how they are looked after. Find out how many people go to the park each year and how much they pay. Prepare a spoken report to give to the rest of the class.

Role–play
Make up a TV or radio programme based on this extract. Build it up through a series of interviews between the reporter and the people involved:

a government official
a safari park owner
a dealer
an RSPCA spokesman
a spokesman for PTES
and so on

Practise each interview carefully and then decide how they should be arranged and presented for an audience.

Defining a horse

Questions to think and talk about

1 What kind of definition of a horse does Bitzer give?
2 Gradgrind says, 'Now . . . you know what a horse is.' Does she?
3 What kind of definition of a horse does Job give?
4 Is one of the definitions better than the other?
5 What kind of a horse has the painter chosen to show?
6 Do any of these include what comes into *your* mind when you think of a horse?

The two extracts raise important points about the nature of writing and register. With some classes it is possible to discuss explicitly the fact that how we write something depends on not only the subject matter but also the audience for, and purpose of, our writing. With other classes such understanding is best left implicit, through the use of exercises such as those that follow.

Language in use

Choose one of these topics:

cycling fast downhill
eating ice cream
going to an exciting football match or film
the first day of the summer holidays

Write two descriptions of it:

a a personal one telling what the experience is really like to you;
b one that Mr Gradgrind would approve of.

Writing

Choose another animal. Write about it in two different ways. You can decide for yourself how to do this, or choose from this list:

a poem
a story written from the creature's viewpoint
a story written from a human viewpoint
an encyclopaedia article
an account of trapping the creature for a zoo

School hymn

discussion

For the unmusical, the tune is 'Buckland', normally associated with the hymn 'Loving Shepherd of Thy Sheep'.

Questions to think and talk about
1 What is the hymn normally sung to this tune?
2 Why did the poet choose this topic when asked to write a school hymn?
3 Do you approve of his choice?
4 In verse 5 he says that the man at the slaughter-house who kills the animals 'Does not strike the blow alone . . .' What does he mean?
5 Why does he end the poem with the words 'Even man'?
6 What is this poem about?

Group discussion
'If you aren't prepared to cut the animal's throat yourself, you shouldn't eat meat.' Do you agree?

Bedtime Story

discussion;
                                                                               writing

Questions to think and talk about
1 Who is telling this story?
2 What has happened to: the world, men, the insects?
3 What is the poet telling us now?

Writing
You are one of the 'wild ones' (verse 4). Tell your story.
or
Write a story about living in a world controlled by giant insects.

Never cry wolf

Group discussion
Farley Mowat set out to study wolves. What did he learn about them in this extract?
1 Read it again.
2 Discuss the question.
3 Write a full answer to it.

Language study
In the passage the author describes how he (like the wolf) marked off his territory by urinating at set intervals. Yet he does not once actually say so. In this way he means to avoid offending anybody. Some people go to great lengths to avoid using words which they consider might give offence. The words they use instead are called euphemisms.

1 What are common euphemisms for: die
                                           lavatory
2 What do these euphemisms mean?
  paying guest
  senior citizen
  funeral director
  refuse collector
  turf accountant
3 What are the advantages and disadvantages of using euphemisms?

Puzzles

Which animal?

1 canaries
2 shark
3 bat

Watching wild animals

As was pointed out in the Introduction, this type of exercise is best tackled in pairs or threes. This is because the process of discussion, of sharing meanings of a text (and how one acquires them) is a vital part of the development of comprehension. It should also be re-emphasized that the pupils are not being asked to guess the actual words used in the original, but to work out suitable words to fill the spaces. In some cases there is only one word. In others there are a number of possibilities. In the answers given below, a few possible variants are given in brackets but there are, of course, others.

1 out
2 plenty (lots)
3 will
4 few
5 occasional
6 possibly (perhaps, maybe)
7 but
8 most
9 secretive
10 only
11 needed
12 but
13 followed
14 small (suburban)
15 several (many)
16 many
17 going (bound)
18 by
19 do
20 you
21 of
22 establish
23 kind
24 in
25 out
26 living
27 for
28 Then (Eventually)
29 of
30 suitable (worthwhile)
31 if (when)
32 for (because)
33 positions
34 obstacles (things)
35 in
36 able
37 them
38 the
39 night
40 two
41 good (sensitive)
42 very (quite)
43 them
44 you
45 downwind
46 be
47 as
48 a
49 position
50 a
51 but
52 you
53 with
54 watch (observe)

Extensions

Further Reading

Fiction Prose

Adams, R.   *Watership Down*
Gallico, P.   *The Snow Goose*
Guillot, R.   *Kpo the Leopard*
Hemingway, E.   *The Old Man and the Sea*
Jarrell, R.   *The Animal Family*
Kipling, R.   *The Jungle Book*
London, J.   *The Call of the Wild*
                     White Fang
Rayner, W.   *Stag Boy*
Roberts, C. G. D.   *Red Fox*
Steinbeck, J.   *The Red Pony*

Non-fiction Prose

Durrell, G.   *My Family and Other Animals* (and others)
Grimble, A.   *A Pattern of Islands*
Maxwell, G.   *Ring of Bright Water*
Mowat, F.   *Never Cry Wolf*
White, T. H.   *The Goshawk*
Williamson, H.   *Tarka the Otter*

Verse

Brownjohn, A.   *Brownjohn's Beasts*
Hughes, T.   *Season Songs*
MacBeth, G. (ed.)   *Penguin Book of Animal Verse*
Masefield, J.   *Reynard the Fox*
Milligan, S.   *A Book of Milliganimals*
Reed, G.   *Out of the Ark*
Watson, J. (ed.)   *A Children's Zoo*

Further Activities

Individual research into life of one animal – from direct observation
                                            – from reading

Further investigation into the ways poets, scientists (and others) describe the same thing.

Writing modern hymns.

SCHOOL 2025

Pupil's book pages 147–156

This Special unit encourages pupils to look at schools of the present with the eyes of both the past and the future. It does this by asking them to envisage what schools will be like in the year 2025. It is divided into the following topic sections:

Buildings

Classrooms and uniforms

Learning

Teachers and discipline

School report

As with other Special units, *School 2025* may be worked on by individuals or groups. One profitable working method is as follows:

1   Pupils begin work on each section in pairs or small groups.
2   They read the source material and look at the illustrations.
3   They discuss the questions.
4   There is a period of general discussion with the whole class, in which groups share their opinions with the others.
5   Pupils then work individually on the Writing Assignments.

Some teachers may feel that the unit explores the subject in more depth and detail than they wish to. Because it is divided into discrete sections, it is perfectly possible to use as much or as little of the material as seems appropriate.

If work is done on loose sheets of paper, these may be collected in folders or put on display to be shared with others in the class.

Section B: Notes

General

This section can be used either for class teaching or for individual reference and practice. Much of the material from Book 1 is repeated since most children need to work over these topics more than once. Whether such repetition is done by the class as a whole, or is a matter for individual study, obviously depends on the teacher and the class.

Pages 158–9   **Nouns, adjectives, verbs, adverbs**

This is a revision unit and the general comments about parts of speech made in Book 1 apply. It is useful, grammatically, to distinguish first between two types of word:

1   'Content' words: nouns, adjectives, verbs, and adverbs. These are words which have a 'content' of meaning which can be established by reference to a dictionary.

2   'Structure' words: prepositions, pronouns, articles, and conjunctions. These have no lexical or meaning content. They are the 'mortar' by means of which the 'bricks' of content words are built up into sentences. All a dictionary can do is tell you *how* they are used, rather than *what* they mean.

It is useful for children to have a working knowledge of the four types of content word, since they need to use dictionaries and the words *noun*, *adjective*, *verb*, and *adverb* are used in dictionaries – *and are useful*. Children are unlikely to look structure words up in a dictionary, and at this stage the technical terms for them are less useful – with the exception of *preposition*, which is introduced in this book.

The difficulty in teaching parts of speech stems from the fact that nouns, adjectives, verbs, and adverbs can be defined both semantically and structurally. The semantic definitions are easier to present – 'A noun is a word used to describe people, places, things, and ideas.' Unfortunately they can be misleading. If a verb is 'used to describe actions', then what about the word 'walk' in the sentence 'I had a pleasant *walk*'? The structural definition is more accurate: each of these four types of word will only fit into certain parts of a sentence. A simple structural definition is quite straightforward in the case of adjectives and adverbs: they can be related to the parts of speech with which they operate. Unfortunately, any kind of simple structural definition of a noun or verb is more or less impossible. Ultimately the teacher has to fall back on practice: if children read enough and talk about the way in which sentences are built up, using the words *noun* and *verb* in their talk, they will develop a working knowledge of what the terms mean. It is the working knowledge that is important, not the ability to reel off definitions learned parrot-fashion.

Pages 160–1 **Sentences**

Again, this is largely a revision unit. Many grammar books categorize sentences into statements, questions, commands, *and exclamations*. Some teachers may like, therefore, to add exclamations for the sake of completeness. This can, however, cause problems. Some exclamations are grammatically indistinguishable from statements:

exclamation: That was fantastic!
statement: That was fantastic.

Others are grammatically difficult to explain:

How fantastic that was!

Here the form seems to be midway between statement and question. In fact the only value of the concept of the exclamation is in the teaching of the exclamation mark, a punctuation mark which most children pick up without teaching (and which many could well be persuaded to drop again).

Pages 162–3 **More about adjectives**

The preceding two units have been concerned respectively with single-word grammar and with sentence grammar. This unit introduces the intermediate concepts of phrase and clause, plus the idea that nouns, adjectives, verbs, and adverbs can be larger components within a sentence than just one word. The phrase/clause distinction of traditional grammar is treated briefly for those teachers who wish to use it. For those who do not, the sentence pattern at the bottom of page 162 can be used in conjunction with exercises A, B, D, without the need to make the distinction explicit.

The definition of a clause contains the words 'a complete verb'. As anyone who has attempted it knows, teaching the meaning of finiteness is not easy. The normal user's concept of finiteness tends to be circular: 'That is not a sentence because it does not contain a finite verb: a finite verb is what every sentence must contain.' Such a user can normally extract from a sentence its finite verb, or make a non-finite form finite by the addition of a suitable auxiliary. What he usually cannot do is to explain this in grammatical terms – and he does not need to be able to. The following grammatical definition is, therefore, included not for teaching purposes, but for the sake of completeness. A finite verb is one which:

a has tense distinction (I walked, I shall walk)
b has mood (you walk, Walk! Were you to walk . . .)
c can occur as the verb in a sentence, and is therefore in agreement in person and number with the subject (I walk, he walks, they walk)

The non-finite forms of the verb are:

a the infinitive (to walk)
b the present participle (walking)
c the past participle (walked)

If one wishes to emphasise the need for a finite verb in a sentence the best line of attack is through the idea of incompleteness.

Additional exercise

These sentences are incomplete because they do not contain a *complete verb*. Write out each sentence and fill the space to complete the verb.
Example: I .... going home now.
Answer: I am going home now.

1 Yesterday my friends .... playing football in the park.
2 Every Saturday I .... to go to see my granny.
3 Our front door .... painted red.
4 Mary .... go to Manchester tomorrow.
5 You .... getting it all wrong.
6 Our team .... beaten all the other schools in the district.
7 I .... to give up French next year and do woodwork instead.
8 When I saw Marie she .... running down the High Street.
9 My sister Alice .... won the cup every year for the past three years.
10 My mother says I .... seen too many TV programmes this week.

Pages 164–5 **Pronouns**

The key sentence in the *Guidelines* is *Do not use a pronoun unless it is clear which noun it refers to*. A pronoun wrongly used, in a situation where it is *not* clear to which noun it refers, is a common cause of confusion in a sentence. Remedial work on such a problem is best attacked at the point of confusion: in the learner's own written work. If possible this should be done by individual explanation. 'This sentence isn't clear. Does "he" refer to "John" or "the shopkeeper"? Then how can you turn the sentence round so that it is clear that you mean "the shopkeeper"?'

Relative pronouns are an area where usage is changing. The traditional rules were as follows:

1 *Restrictive and non-restrictive clauses*
   Relative clauses are of two types: restrictive and non-restrictive. A restrictive clause restricts or defines the noun to which it refers, in such a way that the presence of the relative clause is essential to the sentence. If you remove it you seriously damage or destroy the meaning of the sentence. In the sentence '*The boy* who is sitting over there *is my brother*', the clause 'who is sitting over there' is restrictive. If we remove it we are left with 'The boy is my brother', which is hardly worth saying. This is not true of the non-restrictive relative clause, which does not define and can be removed without such damage: '*John,* whom you met yesterday, *wants to become a doctor*'. Here we can remove 'whom you met yesterday' and the sentence still carries its main sense: 'John wants to become a doctor.' The non-restrictive relative clause 'whom you met yesterday' is merely adding supplementary information.

2 *Relatives in non-restrictive clauses*
Non-restrictive clauses are far less common than restrictive ones and the rules are simpler.

	personal	*impersonal*
subject of clause	who	which
object of clause	whom	which
used with preposition	whom	which

3 *Relatives in restrictive clauses*
Here the rule is more complicated and is subject to change. The traditional rule is:

	personal	*impersonal*
subject of clause	who	which, that
object of clause	whom, zero★	which, that, zero
used with preposition	whom	which

★zero: 'The man *I met yesterday* was a librarian.' The relative clause, 'I met yesterday' is not introduced by any relative pronoun.

Nowadays *that* is frequently used as a personal subject and object relative, although purists will argue that such use is ungrammatical. 'The man *that* remained in the room was staring straight at me.'

A somewhat more straightforward problem is provided by *whose*. Children often need reminding that it is the correct word to use when we wish to say 'of whom' or 'belonging to whom' and that *who's* is a short form of 'who is'. Whether *whose* is used to refer to impersonal nouns, is another area where usage is changing. Sentences such as 'The car *whose* tyre had burst lost the race', are frequent enough to make such usage more or less normal.

Pages 166–9 **Letters**

The information has been kept as simple as possible. Practice changes and develops all the time and obviously textbook examples are a poor substitute for real ones. The presentation of addresses on envelopes is that recommended by the Post Office as at January, 1981. Letters have been set out to conform with this. The style of business letters offered is only one of the many currently in use, and in a school with a commercial studies department, this is a matter that can profitably be discussed. The information about greetings and ending phrases is possibly slightly more formal than is often the case, but business firms vary widely in their practice. The best method is to collect a variety of such letters to show to the class. Teachers who want practice that is more true to life will seek opportunities for children in the class to write real letters to real people. Possible examples might be:

to a local celebrity inviting him/her to talk to the class
to a guest speaker thanking him/her for coming
to a local company asking for a guided tour
a thank-you letter after such a visit
to a member of staff who is away ill or on maternity leave
to an author commenting on one of his/hers books
to a friend who is away from school over a long period
to a company or official body requesting information
to a local paper expressing views about a local issue

Pages 170–3 Punctuation: full stops, capital letters, commas, colons

These four pages are largely a revision of material from Book 1. The section on colons is new. Further punctuation exercises can be devised as needed. Two types are detailed below.

1 *Using examples from the learner's own work*
The teacher takes a passage from the learner's own writing and writes it out, removing all punctuation marks. The child is then asked to re-write the passage – without reference to his own original – putting in the punctuation that he thinks is necessary. This focuses his attention on punctuation directly and specifically. Differences between the two versions can then be discussed with the teacher.

   A similar exercise can be done by a group of pupils, so that the writer on whose work the exercise is based can hear the views of others on how his own work should be punctuated.

2 *Using material from the textbook*
The teacher chooses a passage from Section A, which the class have already read – he then writes it up on the board without punctuation and the children re-write it, adding punctuation. They can then compare their own versions with those of the author. This again can lead to discussion.

Pages 174–5 Apostrophes

This unit is a revision of material in Book 1. As before, all reference to plurals has been avoided, in the hope of avoiding further confusion. The simplification of the rule concerning names that end in 's' has been retained. Some people will argue that one should teach *St James's* and not *St James'*. The answer is that some authorities do indeed say so, but this introduces all the problems of *s's*, and it is worth taking some pains to avoid these.

Pages 176–7 **Script**

This unit is an amplification of the simpler instructions contained in Book 1. It contains more details about the use of stage directions. By now children should be able to make the distinctions between, for example, a radio and a stage script. If facilities are available, a most useful script-writing exercise is to tape-record an improvized conversation, transcribe it verbatim and then turn it into a complete radio or stage script.

Pages 178–9 **Direct speech**

The word *indent* will probably need some explanation.

Pages 180–1 **Using a dictionary**

Children not only need to be encouraged to use dictionaries *at all*: they also need to be shown how to use them *intelligently*. How this is tackled depends on the situation the teacher finds himself in. This can range from having a full set of good dictionaries to a free-for-all in which the children provide their own 'pocket dictionaries', many of which are useless for any serious work. The reference page 180 is deliberately chosen from a 'large' dictionary so as to give the full range of information that a dictionary may provide. Dictionaries used by the children are most unlikely to carry all this information. Although the good ones will carry quite a high proportion of it, they will carry different parts.

The exercises can be a useful reminder for the class, but good dictionary use is a matter of regular and intelligent practice. Once one has got children into the habit of using a dictionary, the next thing one often has to do is to persuade them *not* to use it all the time, or straight away, but to have an intelligent guess at the meaning of a word first. The ability to do this, using the clues of context and word structure is something which has to be fostered. (The next unit, on affixes, deals with one aspect of this.)

In addition to the simple games suggested in *Teacher's Book 1*, a further game can be used. The teacher produces a list of words that are unusual but are in the dictionary used by the children. (For example, *palter, squab, chowder*). The class are then asked to make up and write down their own versions of what they think the words ought to mean – either serious or amusing. Any words they think they know they should, of course, define correctly. When this has been done, the words are discussed with the possible meanings, and then each is looked up in the dictionary. This game is entertaining, but is not just that: it encourages a pleasure in the richness of English vocabulary and a curiosity and willingness to speculate about the strangeness and origins of words.

Pages 182–3 **Parts of a word**

As suggested, the ability to analyse a word and the understanding of prefixes and suffixes is one pre-requisite to beginning to guess intelligently the meaning and spelling of many unknown words. The lists on page 182 can be used to furnish many more exercises of a type similar to exercise D on page 183. Many dictionaries contain appendices listing prefixes and suffixes, with notes on their meaning and usage.

Pages 184–5   **Syllables**

Many teachers find haikus a useful introduction to form in poetry and this work is frequently done in the second year. An essential pre-requisite is an understanding of what a syllable is, hence this unit. Once syllables have been understood, the way is open to look at metre and rhythm in poetry.